Paper Animals

First published in the United States of America by:
Quarry Books, an imprint of
Rockport Publishers, Inc.
146 Granite Street
Rockport, Massachusetts 01966-1299
Telephone: (508) 546-9590
Fax: (508) 546-7141

Distributed to the book trade and art trade in the United States by:
North Light, an imprint of F & W Publications
1507 Dana Avenue
Cincinnati, Ohio 45207
Telephone: (513) 531-2222

ISBN 1-56496-276-8

10 9 8 7 6 5 4 3 2 1

Designer
Kristen Webster
Blue Sky Limited

Photography
Michael Lafferty

Manufactured in Hong Kong by Excel Printing

Paper Animals

Michael G. LaFosse

with best wishes.

1 - 9 - 2004

QUARRY BOOKS
Rockport, Massachusetts

Acknowledgements

I am grateful to Rockport Publishers for allowing me to participate in their paper craft series, and for their encouragement and enthusiasm throughout. I especially wish to thank the following people for lending their talent and courteous help in the production of this book:

Casandra McIntyre and the people at Rugg Road Papers in Boston, for bringing my work to the publisher's attention, and for their continued support to the paper arts community at large; Richard L. Alexander of Alexander Blace & Company in Haverhill, Massachusetts, for his suggestions and support; Shawna Mullen, for reviewing, editing and refining the manuscript, and for ensuring clarity and consistency of instruction; Winnie Danenbarger and Barbara States, for shaping the series concept and making timely suggestions along the way; Rosalie Grattaroti, for her enthusiasm in taking care of the many details that connect author and publisher; Michael Lafferty, for his patient and skillful work on the "how to" and showcase photography; Clark S. Linehan, for his computer composites; and Lynne Havighurst for her artistic direction and for bringing the many elements together beautifully.

Contents

Introduction

The paper animals presented in this book were chosen carefully, with an eye toward offering projects with a range of construction techniques. Each animal is built with a unique folding method, and each method has its own particular strengths. Design tips and a gallery section round out the projects and demonstrate the many possibilities of the papers and templates provided.

Printed purple templates and extra paper sets are provided for all of the projects in this book. Trace the templates to create animals from any material you choose. Or adapt these animal shapes to design creatures of your own.

Enjoy!
—Michael G. LaFosse

How to Use This Book

Each project begins with a list of materials and a picture of the finished animal. For your first attempts, the papers provided are marked with folding lines; the templates in the back of the book can be traced to make an endless supply of animal patterns. To get the best possible results, the three most important things to keep in mind are: cut slowly and carefully, fold precisely, and get to know the key on page 11. The key explains the fold lines and arrows (known as the Yoshizawa/Randlet standardized origami system) that accompany each drawing in this book. If you are already familiar with this system of folding notation you will feel right at home; otherwise, spend a few minutes learning to recognize the symbols and to understand the terminology.

Begin by cutting out all paper elements for the desired project from the supply sheets provided at the back of the book. Use sharp, comfortable scissors and take your time. An X-Acto knife makes clean work of detailed areas. Protect your work surface by placing a piece of cardboard under your work if you are cutting with a blade. You will need a ruler or some other straightedge for most projects, along with a tool such as a letter opener to score fold lines on the back of the animal elements. Scoring the paper first will make folding on the lines much easier.

Carefully study the step-by-step photos, to visually check your work. It is often helpful to look ahead to the next diagram or photo to see the results of a fold in advance. Take time to make neat, accurate folds.

Though adhesives are not always necessary, you may wish to make your creations last longer by adding a little white glue or paste at key contact points. Apply adhesives sparingly and neatly, and have a damp cloth handy to wipe away spills.

Purple tracing templates are provided for each project, so that you can make additional animals from whatever material you choose. The showcase at the end of the book offers variations on each animal for added inspiration.

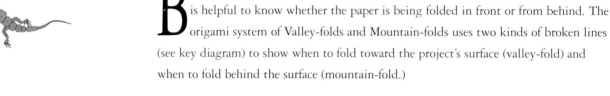

Glossary & Key

B ecause the illustrations can show only a segment of a project's folding procedure, it is helpful to know whether the paper is being folded in front or from behind. The origami system of Valley-folds and Mountain-folds uses two kinds of broken lines (see key diagram) to show when to fold toward the project's surface (valley-fold) and when to fold behind the surface (mountain-fold.)

Valley-fold - Relative to the displayed view of the paper being folded, a valley-fold is always folded in front of the project's surface. If you were to unfold a valley-fold you would see a valley-crease, which dents into the paper's surface forming a valley.

Mountain-fold - Relative to the displayed view of the paper being folded, a mountain-fold is always folded behind the project's surface. If you were to unfold a mountain-fold you would see a mountain-crease, which rises up from the paper's surface forming a mountain ridge.

Various types of arrows help make the folding instructions even clearer. These arrows are easy to understand with a quick study of the illustrated key. Whenever you see the repeat arrow in a diagram, you must apply the demonstrated folding procedure to all indicated parts of the project.

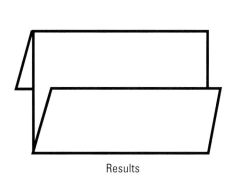

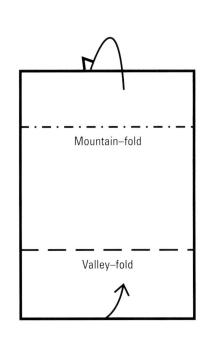

Mountain–fold

Valley–fold

Results

Standard Symbols

Valley-fold

Mountain-fold

Directional Arrows

In Front   Behind

Turn Model Over

Insert/Apply Pressure   Cut

Repeat

Enlarged View

Painting and Decorating

Whether you choose plain or patterned paper, the animal shapes in these projects are distinct enough to stand on their own. If you would like to decorate the animals to make them more realistic or more fanciful, you can use acrylic paint, inks, markers, crayons, stencils, appliqués, and even monoprinting. A few favorite decorating techniques are illustrated here, use them as inspiration to create beautiful designs of your own.

Add Shine

Apply a rainbow of shimmering luster with iridescent acrylic paint. These paints come in many colors, and are permanent and fade-resistant. For best results, paint a dark base-coat first. Paint on a smooth, seamless field of iridescence, or try using brushes, rollers, sponges, or rags to make textured and mottled effects. This paint works especially well to decorate the frog and the lizard projects.

Sponge Paint

Daubing on paint makes it easy to produce textures and multicolored effects. Use a sponge or wadded rag to dab or streak broken areas of color over the paper. Use a separate sponge or rag for each color and apply dark colors first. Experiment with smudging or scraping the applied paints while they are wet. Acrylic tube colors are the best choice for this technique, since they are flexible and water resistant when dry. Use only non-toxic colors around children. This technique is great for decorating paper turtles and fish.

Add Texture

You can copy the texture of many different surfaces with the crayon rubbing technique. Place paper over the chosen texture and rub with a crayon. Oil pastels, colored pencils, and varying the amount of pressure and shape of stroke will produce different effects. A plastic mesh bag, such as a grocery fruit bag, is wonderful for making "reptile skin" textures.

Japanese Style

What better way to ornament koi than with a Japanese painting style, brush (fude), and ink (sumi). To get this effect, paint on heavyweight, bright white, absorbent paper. Black, crimson and vermilion inks are best for koi. Prepare a liquid painting solution, load the brush with ink or paint, and touch the tip to the surface of the paper. Allow the ink or paint to bleed into the paper as you go: aim for rounded shapes with slightly soft edges. You may want to practice on ordinary newsprint first.

Appliqués

Appliqués decorate paper with very precise, rich patterns. Here, colored shapes for a parrot are cut out, then pasted in place. This can be done before or after cutting out the final paper form. Draw a light pencil line to indicate the proper placement of the various elements.

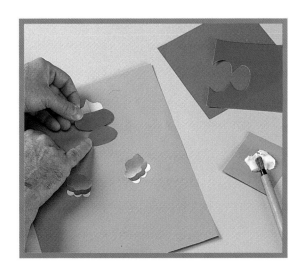

Monoprints

1 Monoprinting can generate a wide variety of effects on paper. The basic materials needed are substrate, paint, paper and a burnishing tool. Many types of surfaces and paints will work to create monoprints: here, we used a stiff plastic board and acrylic tube paints. To get this effect, apply color in parallel rows directly from the tube and smear with a piece of cardboard.

2 Place substrate-coated paper face-down on the cardboard and rub with the back of a spoon to impress the paint on the surface of the paper.

3 Peel the paper up and let dry. It is possible to obtain several prints from one prepared surface.

Stencils

1 Stencils will also produce rich patterns and textures on paper. You can color or paint stencils by hand, or use spray paint for a fast finish. To stencil with spray paint, sandwich the chosen paper between the stencil and an "over-spray" sheet. The overspray sheet will protect your work area. Make sure that the stencil lies completely flat against the surface of the paper to be decorated. Spray paint in an even, controlled manner—or experiment by spraying short bursts, long and narrow bands, circular patterns, etc.

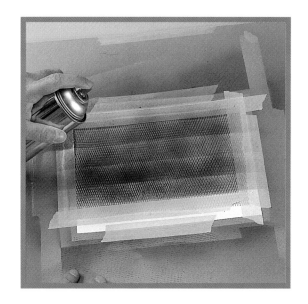

2 Each method will yield different results from the same stencil. Carefully remove the stencil and paper from the overspray sheet and allow to dry. Always work in well-ventilated areas and use a respirator if suggested by the manufacturer.

Paper Frog

Frogs and toads figure in many traditional tales and legends all over the world. Their amusing, odd shapes make them charming and sometimes irresistible. Frogs have been fashioned from every kind of material: gold, silver, semiprecious stones, wood, porcelain, fabric, plastic, and of course, paper. Some people like to collect frogs, others may keep at least one for good luck.

The Japanese word for frog is *kaeru*, which sounds just like the Japanese word for "return home" and can be taken to mean: "Hopefully you will return." A gift of the likeness of a frog means the same thing: Give these paper frogs to friends as keepsakes that invite a return visit; or as mementos to wish travelers safe return home.

How to Build a Paper Frog

The frog is easy to make and fun to decorate. Real frogs come in every color of the rainbow, so anything goes for paper frogs. Bright or drab, speckled or striped, these frogs will liven up a table, bookcase, house plant, or windowsill.

    Printed paper, to make both pond frogs and tree frogs, is provided in the back of the book. Try your hand at decorating paper frogs with appliqués and paint. Finished examples in the showcase chapter show variations you can make with this pattern; you may also want to consult illustrated field guides on the subject of amphibians. This project can be adapted to make paper toads, salamanders, and beetles.

Materials

- *Frog paper elements*

- *Scissors and/or X-Acto Knife*

- *Paste or glue stick*

- *Brush for applying paste*

Design Tips

- *Use sharp scissors or an X-Acto knife with a fresh blade to cut out the paper pattern. This will give you cleaner edges and a better-looking model.*
- *When removing paper pieces, cut from the back side of the paper provided. Cut just inside the outlines, and fold exactly on the indicated crease lines.*
- *Use very dark paper decorated with acrylic-based, iridescent paint to make frogs that look wet and slick.*
- *Create unusual jewelry by making frogs from foil or heavy aluminum embossing-sheets and then backing with a brooch pin.*

1 Score or valley-crease along the dashed lines on the underside of the frog pattern. This will give the frog's back a rounded shape. You can vary the degree of roundness by changing the angle of the folds.

2 Cut along the dotted lines to release the hind legs.

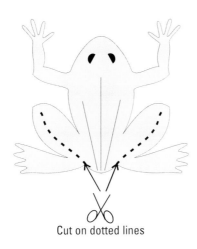

Cut on dotted lines

3 Valley-fold the front legs inward, horizontally across the underside of the pattern.

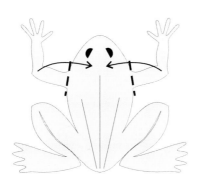

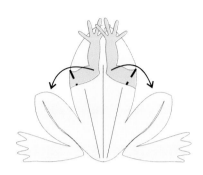

4 Valley-fold the front legs at a downward angle away from the shoulder area.

5 Form "elbows" in the front legs by mountain- and valley-folding a V-shaped set of pleats, as shown. The completed folds will allow you to position the frog's legs in a variety of ways for a natural pose.

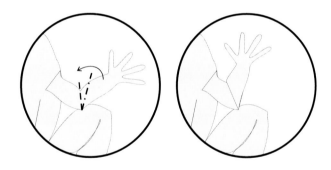

6 Using an X-Acto knife, cut a semi-circular line around the eyes of the frog. Turn the model over.

7 Fold the eyelids up, away from this side of the paper. You can shape the paper lids with a slight curve or roundness. Apply a small dot of glue to the heel of each of the frog's back feet.

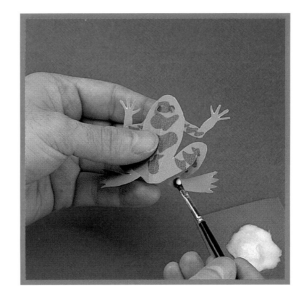

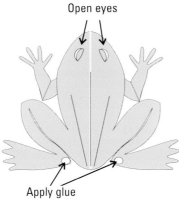

Open eyes

Apply glue

8 Glue the heels under the rump of the frog to make the hind legs rounded and three-dimensional. Valley-fold the hind legs at the waistline and adjust the all-over shape of the frog.

Glue heels under rump

9 The finished frog.

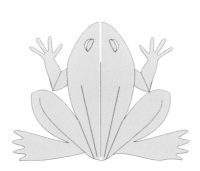

Paper Sea Turtle

There are more than two hundred species of turtles in the world. They live on land, in freshwater ponds, and in the sea. Since turtles are reputed to live a great many years, they are often used as symbols of longevity and security. Giving a gift with the figure of a turtle on it is a nice way to mark a christening, a wedding, or the opening of a new business. Turtles have a friendly charm, and people have reported feeling soothed simply by watching turtles. Who could possibly feel agitated when the pace of life is set by the turtle? Would that every day could be so calm.

Materials

- *Sea turtle box paper elements*

- *Scissors and/or X-Acto Knife*

- *Paste or glue stick*

- *Brush for applying paste*

How to Build a Paper Sea Turtle Box

This turtle is also an unusual box that is handy for keeping small items on a desk or dresser top. You may choose to build just the top half of the sea turtle box—to make a wonderful gift package ornament or to string on a mobile. Use the blue template at the end of the book to make sea turtles that coordinate with gift wrap, wallpaper, or any kind of paper you choose. The turtle is a symbol of wisdom, and the paper turtle box is a wise addition to any repertoire of gift creations.

Design Tips

- *Use paste or a glue stick instead of liquid glue: Paste will not warp paper as easily as liquid glue, and its slow drying time allows more time to position elements.*

- *Work on only one tab at a time when making the base of the box. You will have better control if you proceed in order, one tab after the other, around the box perimeter.*

- *Center the box under the turtle-shell lid, so that the shell rim extends evenly beyond the edges of the box. Pre-flex the hinge before attaching the lid.*

- *Heavyweight paper with a surface texture works best for making the turtle box. Lightweight paper is fine for mobiles and package ornaments.*

1 Mountain- and valley-fold the head and limbs of the sea turtle under the edge of the shell, as shown; you can swivel these parts to effect various swimming postures and to give each turtle more personality.

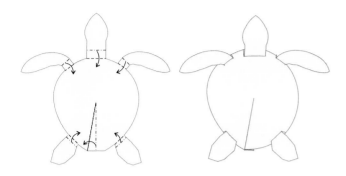

2 Round the shell of the turtle by mountain-folding a small ridge of paper at the back end. Make sure that no white paper remains visible on the other side of the shell. Secure folds with a little paste.

3 Pre-crease all the indicated fold lines on the paper for the box base. All but the tabs on the T-shaped extensions are valley-folds.

4 Valley-fold the T-shaped tab extensions inward. The top edge of each extension should touch the octagonal outline of the floor of the box.

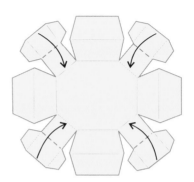

5 Apply paste to the outside of each of the eight tabs. The tabs to be pasted can be recognized by their slanted edges. There are two tabs on each of the T-shaped extensions.

Apply paste

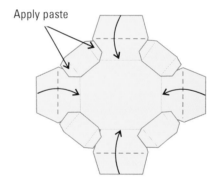

6 Press each pasted tab against its adjacent wall edge and fold the remaining extended edges of paper over all to cover. Press firmly to seal. The finished box bottom will have sloping sides and be somewhat dish-shaped.

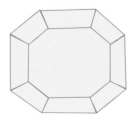

7 Fold the paper hinge and paste one half to the inside of one of the long walls of the box bottom.

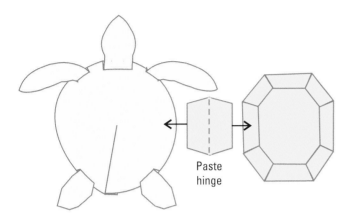

Paste hinge

8 Paste the other half of the paper hinge to the inside of the sea turtle shell. Align the box bottom with the center of the shell, so that the turtle's shell is centered over the box when the lid is closed.

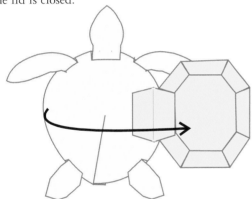

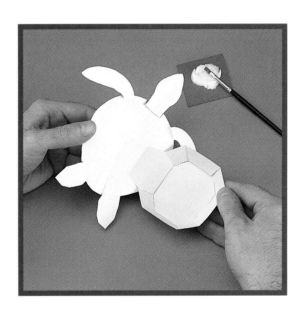

9 The finished sea turtle box.

Paper Lizard

Lizards and snakes are reptiles, cold-blooded animals that require warmth from the sun to get their day started. You may see these animals sunning themselves on rocks or stumps as if posing for a picture to be taken. Once startled, however, the show is quickly over and they flee for cover in the blink of an eye.

Salamanders, which resemble lizards in some ways, are amphibians and are more closely related to frogs and toads. They prefer watery or damp environments, and have no scales or claws. Because salamanders and lizards are shaped so similarly, you can adapt the same paper pattern to make either animal.

How to Build a Paper Lizard

This lizard is modeled after a popular toy: You can assemble it without legs to make a snake. Use this pattern to make paper or plastic lizards, salamanders, and snakes of every description. Use faux leather or crocodile and bright fabrics to make wonderful, durable versions of these toys, too. Decorate with paint, sequins, glitter, and beads for fanciful and elaborate effects.

All of the projects in this book are great inclusions in a mobile, and the lizard is no exception: it will wiggle and sway in gentle air currents. You can also make marionette lizards by attaching support threads to the feet.

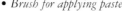

Materials

- *Lizard paper elements*

- *Scissors and/or X-Acto Knife*

- *Paste or glue stick*

- *Brush for applying paste*

Design Tips

- *Feel free to trim any paper that does not fit during assembly. The pattern is flexible and allows for variation.*

- *You can paste the leg elements on the top or bottom of any body segment, instead of assembling by the illustrated method. This simplifies construction and yields a different finished effect.*

- *As a shortcut, try simply cutting out the shape of the head at the eye area—instead of folding over the extra paper. You can then glue the simple paper head to the inside upper surface of the first body segment..*

- *Spread the body segments further apart for a more wiggly lizard.*

1 Work so that the lizard's face remains on the outside of the paper. Pre-crease all the lines on the lizard head paper and fold it in half, short edge to short edge. All but one of the pre-creases will be valley-folds. The short distance across the paper between the notches is a mountain-fold—it will be pushed into the larger fold to form a pointed nose.

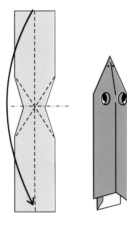

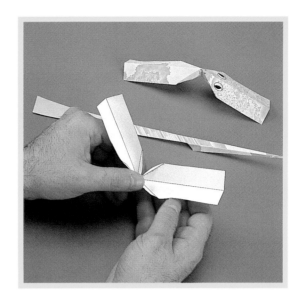

2 Before you attach the lizard's head to the tail, be sure that the edge of the tail with the raised "keel" is upper-most, as shown. Fold the paper over to form a neat edge: this is the top of the lizard's backbone. Apply paste to the wide end of the tail and slide it into the back of the lizard's head. Press the pasted papers together and flatten from side to side with your thumb.

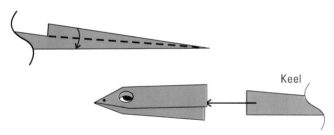

Keel

3 Mountain- and valley-fold each of the eight body seg-ments, which are numbered on the underside. The number sequence begins at the head and ends with segment eight at the tail. Apply paste to each rounded tab just before you attach it to the tail strip.

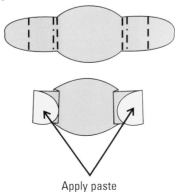

Apply paste

4 Pay careful attention to the proper attachment of the body segments. First, press a pasted tab on one side of the tail strip and secure. Bring the remaining tab around to the other side of the strip and attach it. Body segment number one should cover the joint between the head and the tail strip.

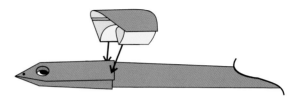

5 Shape the front limbs of the lizard by mountain folding as shown, then paste the limbs to the tail strip behind and slightly underneath the first body segment. Push the limbs under the body segment as far as possible without dislodging the segment.

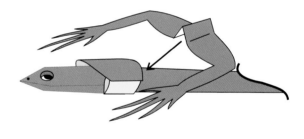

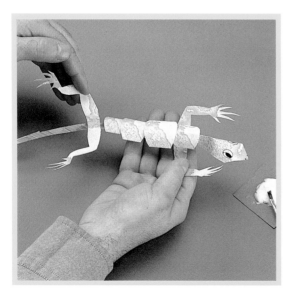

6 Add body segments 2 through 4 in the same manner. Be sure that body segment number 2 covers the front limb attachment area. Add the hind limbs after segment 4, nesting them in the same manner as the front limbs. Attach the remaining body segment pieces.

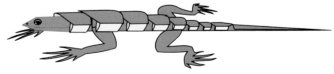

7 Once the hind limbs and the remaining body segments are in place, you can add detail by shaping each of the limbs: Make a few simple creases down the middle line of each limb, and accent "shoulder" and "elbow" joints with creases, too.

8 This flexible model can be posed in many ways.

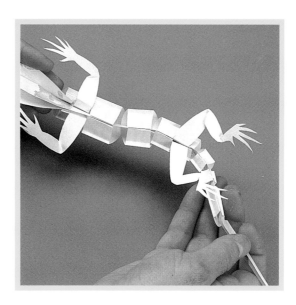

9 The finished lizard.

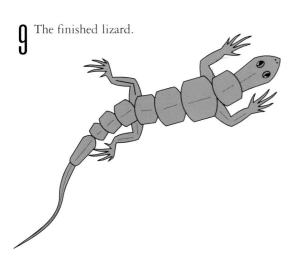

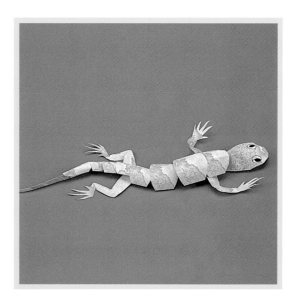

Paper Koi

In Japan, the carp symbolizes strength. Colorful kites resembling carp are hoisted each year in celebration of Boy's Day, a national Japanese holiday. The Japanese treasure the beauty of carp, and have traditionally bred many beautiful ornamental varieties, called koi. Today, people all over the world are discovering the beauty of koi—raising them in aquariums, garden pools, and simple backyard ponds. Any garden is greatly enhanced by a contemplative pool stocked with healthy koi. You can stock an indoor garden with these charming paper substitutes until the real ones arrive.

Materials

- *Koi paper elements*

- *Scissors and/or X-Acto Knife*

- *Paste or glue stick*

- *Brush for applying paste*

How to Build Paper Koi

Koi are considered very intelligent and friendly fish, and koi fanciers have bred some exceptionally beautiful varieties. Since they are popular features of many public gardens, it is likely you will be able to find some live koi for inspiration.

With a few sheets of paper and some paint you can create your own paper koi pond at home. Decorating paper koi with signature patterns of crimson, black, and gold is nearly as much fun as building them. You can paint the paper before you cut out the pattern, or you may prefer to compose the design on a finished, blank paper model. Either way you will want variety in the collection, so try both.

Design Tips

- *When pasting the rear ventral fins to each side of the keel in Step 4, keep the sides of the body, near the tail, rounded as you paste. The body will remain nicely rounded once secured in this way.*

- *When bending the head down in Step 6, remember to just hide the paper tabs with the gill covers—no further.*

- *When arranging groups of paper fish, curl the fins in a variety of ways, especially the tail fin.*

- *If you want to paint your koi, construct them from very white, slightly absorbent paper, such as watercolor paper. Apply paint with a light touch.*

1 Use an X-Acto knife to cut carefully on the dotted lines for the gills and center slot of the koi. DO NOT cut on the dashed lines.

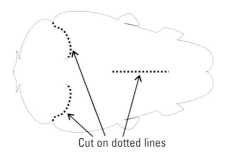

Cut on dotted lines

2 Mountain-fold the fins flanking the paper shape, as shown, and valley-fold the middle from the back end to the center slot.

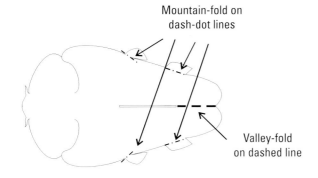

Mountain-fold on
dash-dot lines

Valley-fold
on dashed line

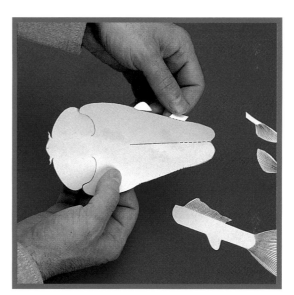

3 Apply paste to both sides of the indicated keel of the fin, as shown. Keeping the body paper flat, slip the top (dorsal) fin through the center slot that you cut in Step 1.

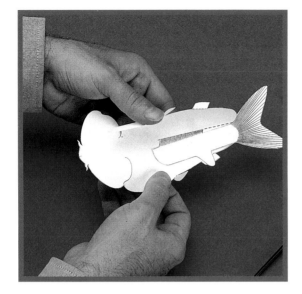

4 Fold the koi body paper in half and over the fin assembly. Keep the sides of the paper somewhat rounded as you attach the small, rectangular set of fins to the pasted keel. Carefully check the appearance of the koi at this point. The body should be conical and trim.

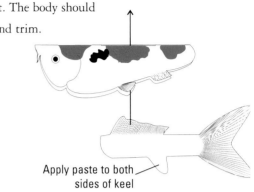

Apply paste to both sides of keel

5 Trim any excess keel paper protruding from the pasted fin area. Fold back the rounded tabs near the gill covers, as shown.

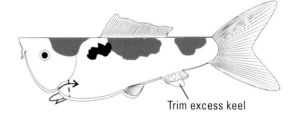

Trim excess keel

6 Apply paste to the outside of the folded tabs and bend the head just enough to attach the gill covers to the folded tabs.

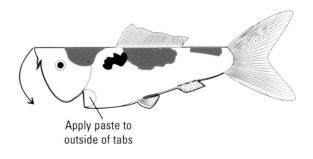

Apply paste to outside of tabs

7 The effect is a graceful, rounded fold for the slope of the koi's head. The gills should stand slightly open.

8 Apply paste to the tabs of the pectoral fins (they are labeled) and attach them to the inside walls of the open front, below and just behind the head. You can adjust these fins to any position that suits you.

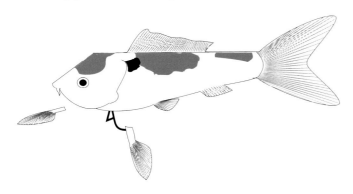

9 The finished koi.

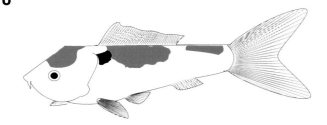

Paper Zebra

Describe a zebra in three words, and you will probably come up with: wild, African horse. Contemplate each of these three words and you will begin to understand the zebra. Wild: There is something inherently primitive and untamed about zebras. African: Zebras live in the wild only in Africa, that huge and most exotic of continents. Horse: We connect with the zebra because we are so familiar with its cousin, the domestic horse. While this gives us some insight into zebras, their mystical quality remains. Even as still paper forms, they look exotic.

How to Build a Paper Zebra

The construction method demonstrated for the zebra adapts for creating most other four-legged animals: dogs, giraffes, elephants, cats, etc. If you choose to make a zebra and not a horse, don't be put off by trying to match up the stripes: The pattern is so busy that it hides slight imperfections in construction. You can scale the pattern up or down on a copy machine, to make very large or miniature animals. Paper is provided for making one zebra and one horse. You can create ponies by shrinking the horse pattern slightly. The zebra is suited to constructing in herds—especially if you include a few small zebra colts.

Materials

- *Zebra paper elements*
- *Scissors and/or X-Acto Knife*
- *Paste or glue stick*
- *Brush for applying paste*
- *Straightedge*
- *Letter opener*

Design Tips

- *For practice, make multiple photocopies of the cutout and read through the steps before you begin.*
- *Experiment with poses for the head and legs. Consult photographs of horses and zebras for ideas.*
- *After final assembly, trim the bottoms of the hooves so that they are all even and neat. This is the best way to adjust the stance.*
- *Use glue or paste to keep the body closed and the legs close together.*

1 With an X-Acto knife, cut open a slot for the mane as shown. Valley-fold the leg and neck tabs in. Trim the bottom of the hooves if necessary. Turn the model over.

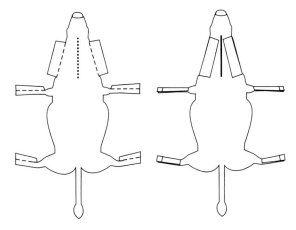

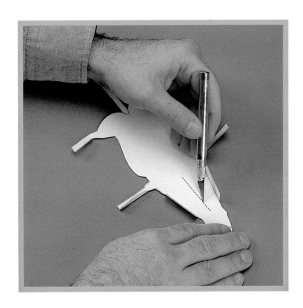

2 Using the X-Acto knife, cut around the outer edges of the ears to partially separate them from the head.

3 To form the rump, mountain- and valley-fold the hindquarters on the lines indicated in the drawing.

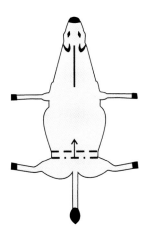

4 Mountain- and valley-fold the forequarters, as shown, to form the shoulders.

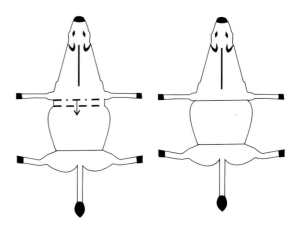

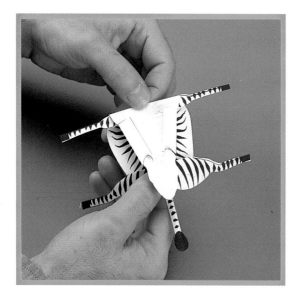

5 Fold the neck back against the body. The fold line should run straight across the front line of the forelegs.

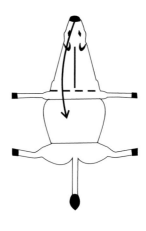

6 Look carefully at the dashed lines on the underside of the neck in the illustration. Using a straightedge and letter opener, pre-crease lines like those on the model. The angle of these folds is adjustable, so there is no precise placement. After pre-creasing the paper, fold the neck forward while folding the zebra in half lengthwise. The result is illustrated in the drawing in Step 7.

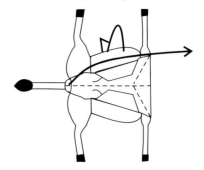

7 Bend the head downward while allowing the ears to rotate upward. Once you are happy with the angle, gently press in the sides of the head to crease it in place. Here, too, you can make adjustments.

8 Insert the mane through the slot in the back of the neck. Secure it in place with a little glue. For added effect, you can snip the mane with scissors. Bend the tail down.

9 The finished zebra. The neck can be adjusted in different postures.

Paper Gliding Bird

P aper gliders become even more fun when you can take pride in the fact that you have built them yourself. Kites and toy gliders come in all shapes and colors, but none are more inspiring than those that resemble some wonderful bird, plying the winds and seeming to come to life in the breeze of a sunny day.

When building a new glider, always take care to fold very neatly. The number one axiom for best flight performance is balance! Once you understand the basics of good flight performance, you will want to make flocks of new flying creatures. Experience is the best teacher. Don't waste any more time—test your wings!

How to Build a Paper Gliding Bird

T his graceful glider is a fun to make and even more fun to fly. Use the gliding bird as a party favor, or build a mobile and display a whole flock. Quick to make from any kind of paper, lightweight paper makes the best gliders.

Once you master the simple method of construction, you can adapt this pattern to make gliders of your own devising. The front edges of the wings are thick, folded layers of paper for stiffness. The body of the bird also has layered folds, to weight the front and to provide stable seating for the wings. Paste or glue is not needed for assembly, but we recommend it for permanence.

Materials

- *Gliding bird paper elements*
- *Scissors and/or X-Acto Knife*
- *Paste, glue stick or tape*
- *Brush for applying paste*

Design Tips

- *Be sure to cut neatly to preserve the symmetry of the wings. The wings control the bird's balance during flight.*
- *For faster flights, weight the front of the bird by adding a few pieces of tape.*
- *Before launching, check that the wings and tail are evenly set and without any twists or dents.*
- *Small birds, made out of reasonably stiff paper, fly the best. Experiment with different launching techniques. Basically, any way that you are able to get this bird into the air should produce a gliding flight.*

1 Begin by valley-folding the leading edges of the wing
 paper to make them dense and rigid. You should fold the
narrow, flanking edges first, then the two large center areas.
The larger edges will overlap the smaller edges and hold
them in place. You can use glue or tape to keep the folded,
leading edges in place.

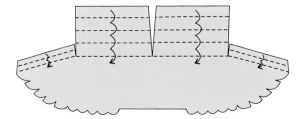

2 Valley-fold the outer wing areas, as shown. Mountain-
 fold the center of the wing. The resulting M-shape of the
final wing will provide additional stability in flight.

3 Begin to shape the body by mountain- and valley-
 folding the part of the body strip closest to the tail.
Light-colored dashed lines are printed on the paper as a
guide. The result of the first two folds will look like the
figure in step 4.

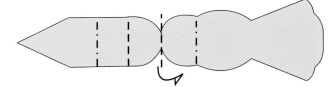

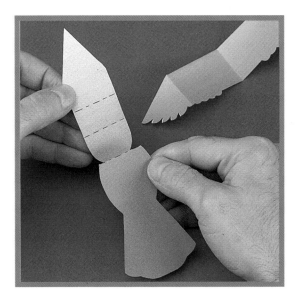

4 Valley and mountain-fold the remaining portion of the strip. The folds of paper at the front of the body provide the extra weight that will pull the model forward, through the air.

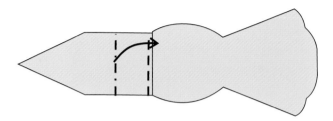

5 Mountain-fold the two indicated corners of the layered paper as shown, so that they disappear under the square edge. This helps to lock these layers in place. Mountain-fold the tail edges to form the tail stabilizers.

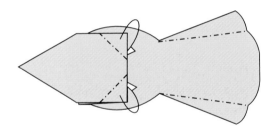

6 Form the bird's head and beak area by mountain- and valley-folding the pointed end of the body strip. There is no ideal placement for these particular folds, so just use your judgment. Mountain-fold the smaller side corners, as indicated, to make the shape trim.

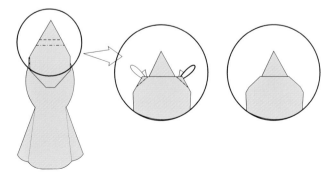

7 Valley-fold the body in half, lengthwise, to make a V-shape channel. This channel forms a stabilizing keel and a center valley to cradle the wings of the bird.

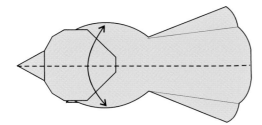

8 Insert the paper wings under the heavy folded paper edge of the head. You can use a bit of glue or tape to secure the assembly, but it is often not necessary if you have folded the paper crisply and neatly.

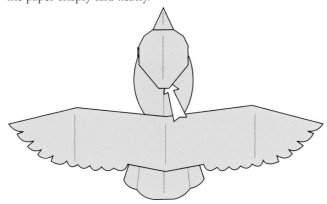

9 The finished gliding bird. To launch, hold on to the front center edge of the wing assembly and toss the gliding bird straight up, over your head in a backhand manner. The idea is to get the paper bird high in the air, where it will recover from a graceful loop and glide slowly to the ground.

Paper Parrot

Parakeets, macaws, cockatoos and lorikeets are all members of the parrot family. They have hooked beaks and are among the most agile of birds. Often referred to as the clowns of the bird world, parrots are very entertaining and have long been favored as pets.

If you have ever had a parrot, you know that they can be very particular birds. When you try your hand at making parrots from paper, keep in mind that paper sometimes behaves like a parrot and will try to have its own way. Your results may display some of your intentions and some of the paper's! Which is all for the best, since each paper parrot is bound to be unique.

How to Build a Paper Parrot

T he unusual construction of this bird allows you to pose the model with a sunflower seed in its beak. You can modify the beak and tail design to make other members of the parrot family, such as macaws and parakeets; or add a crest to make a cockatiel or a cockatoo. Parrots are among the most colorful of birds—sporting plumage in vivid hues of emerald, azure, ruby, gold, and amethyst—so select paper colors accordingly.

Substitute paper-stiffened fabric for plain paper, or decorate your creations with appliqués instead of paint. Make miniature parrots to use as a brooch or earrings.

Materials

- *Parrot paper elements*

- *Scissors and/or X-Acto Knife*

- *Paste or glue stick*

- *Brush for applying paste*

Design Tips

- *Use an adhesive, such as paste, that allows a little extra time for adjustments. This will give you flexibility in creating the best balance and expression.*
- *When cutting out the pattern, be sure to cut all the way to the end of the line on each side of the neck area. This is important for shaping the head.*
- *For more colorful birds, decorate paper with appliqués.*
- *You can modify the tail and beak shape or even add a crest to create different types of tropical birds.*

1 Begin on the underside of the paper. Pre-crease the indicated mountain- and valley-folds in the shoulder and beak areas. You can make these folds directly or score them first with a straightedge and letter opener.

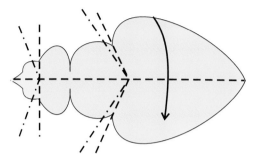

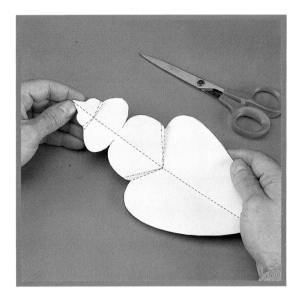

2 When the shoulder and beak areas begin to bend inward, valley-fold along the center line and fold the model in half. Turn the model over.

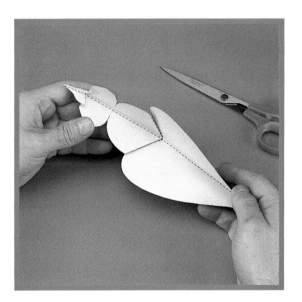

3 This view of the back shows the outside shape of the shoulders. Notice that the model is left somewhat open.

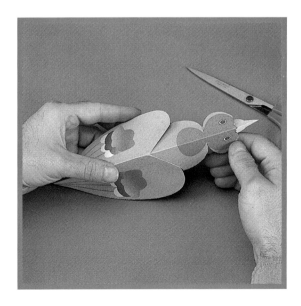

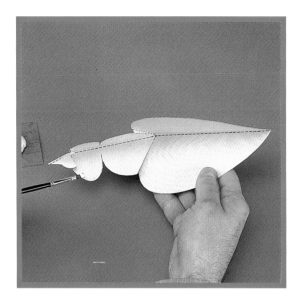

4 Apply a little paste to the inside of each "cheek" area, in preparation for securing the head. The cheeks will attach to the outside of the neck paper once the head is in position.

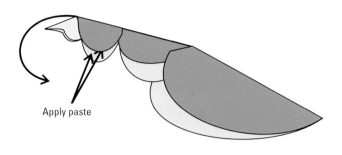

Apply paste

5 Bend the head downward and secure it in the desired position by pressing the pasted paper to the outside of the neck. You can alter the expression of the bird by changing the angle of its head.

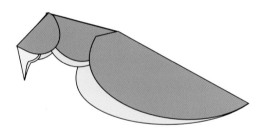

6 The solid yellow paper forms the belly, breast, and lower bill of the parrot. Begin by pre-creasing the indicated mountain- and valley-folds at the narrow end of the paper, as shown. If you carefully crease only on the dashed lines provided and are sure to distinguish between valley- and mountain-folds, you will have no trouble folding the lower part of the bill.

7 Now work the paper at the other end by mountain- and valley-folding between the V-notched areas. The parrot's legs will protrude from each of these V-notches.

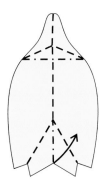

8 Fold the belly/breast area in half, allowing the beak paper to be at an angle on the outside and the leg area to fold inside.

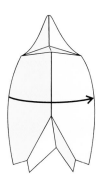
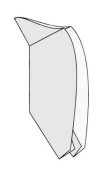

9 Preparing the tail/leg paper is as easy as folding a paper fan. Mountain- and valley-fold it on the indicated dashed lines and compress it to make a narrow shape. Turn the paper over to display the brighter side.

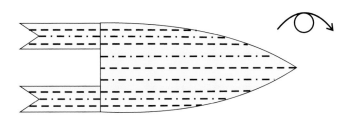

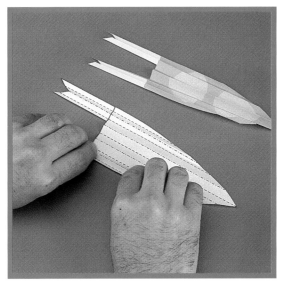

10 Fold the two yellow leg forms down on each side of the green paper where they join the top of the tail.

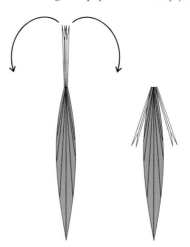

11 Apply paste to each side of the V-notched section on the lower inside of the yellow body form. Attach the top of the pale green (underside) surface of the tail form to the pasted edges of the V-notched paper. The two pasted edges will fit easily into the center valley-fold on the underside of the tail. Adjust the angle of the tail to your liking, but be sure to place each leg in its corresponding smaller V-notch opening, located to the right and left sides of the tail seating. Fold the body closed.

Apply paste

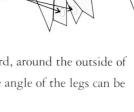

12 Fold each leg forward, around the outside of the lower body. The angle of the legs can be adjusted.

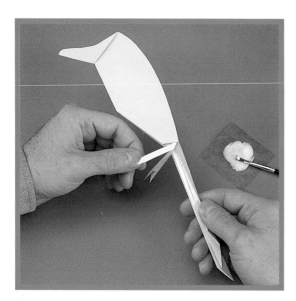

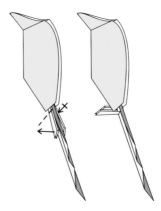

13 Fit body and tail/beak sections together before applying paste, to determine whether any adjustments are needed. Apply paste to the inside of the neck paper and fit the body and tail/beak sections together. Press all layers together to secure. The body can be rounded after the paste has set.

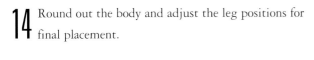

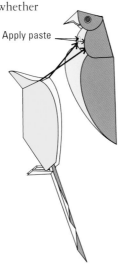

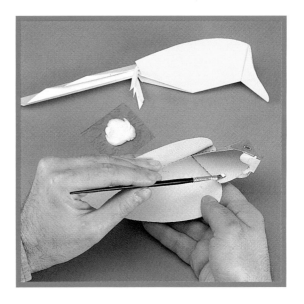

14 Round out the body and adjust the leg positions for final placement.

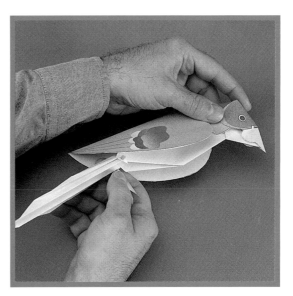

15 The finished parrot can be perched on the edge of a table or bookcase. Use wire or tape to make a more permanent display.

Paper Bat

Bats are certainly one of the most amazing and misunderstood of mammals. Perhaps it is their secretive, nocturnal habits that cause concern, or maybe it is their odd form. One need only take a closer look at these wonderful animals to begin to like them. Fortunately for bats and people alike, society is realizing the important role bats play in nature: Insect-eating bats help keep bug populations down; and pollen-eating and fruit-eating bats are vital to many plants. Many people have even built bat-houses to offer roosting sites for mosquito-eating bats. Paper bats are less intimidating than the real models, though not as effective against insects.

How to Build a Paper Bat

I n China, the bat has long been a symbol of good luck. The image of the bat is a popular motif in oriental pottery, fabric and building decoration. A dwelling with bats is considered fortunate.

The origami bat is the most challenging of the projects in this book, but it is worth the effort. This sought-after design is very popular: Even people who don't find the image of a bat endearing warm up to these charming fellows. It is also, of course, the perfect Halloween decoration or package ornament.

Materials

- *Bat paper elements*

- *Scissors and/or X-Acto Knife*

- *Paste or glue stick*

Design Tips

- *Always use paper that is the same color on both sides. If you have square origami paper that is colored on one side and white on the other, simply fold it in half, corner to corner, with the color on the outside; you will now have a triangle of the proper dimensions and colored on both sides.*

- *If you are using heavyweight paper, dampen it first with a sponge and then fold; when the paper dries, the folds will remain. Wet-folding is also a good way to add expressive touches to your work.*

- *Make a small hole in the center of the top of the head and add a loop of thread to make bat ornaments.*

- *Experiment by modifying the wings, ears, and faces of these bats, to make models that are large and scary, or small and delightful.*

1 Cut a square of paper diagonally in half, to make a
triangle of the proper proportions to begin this project.
This correct type of triangle has one square corner and two
45-degree angle corners. Any size will do.

Valley-fold the triangle in half by bringing the two
45-degree angles together as shown. Unfold. This creates a
centerline. Valley-fold all three corners to meet at the end
of this center line where it touches the center of one of the
triangle's sides. Unfold. You will now have a set of valley-
creases, as pictured.

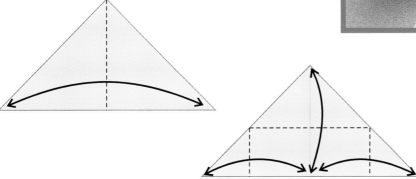

2 Valley-fold the two, 45-degree angle corners to the
square corner. Turn the paper over. Notice how this
square shape has two open edges and two folded edges.
Focus on the two folded edges of the square for the next
step: Fold each of these edges to the center line and allow
the triangular points from the underside to rotate around to
the front of the paper. The model should now resemble the
photo. Pay particular attention to the mountain-creases,
which bisect each of the triangular shapes in front.

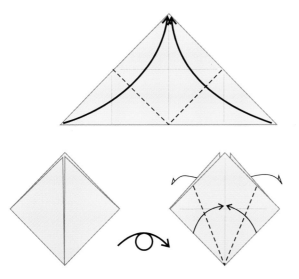

3 Grasp one of the mountain-creases, align it with the center of the model, and valley-fold the paper between the mountain-crease and the center line of the model. Do the same with the other mountain-crease. Mountain- and valley-fold the resulting paper triangles. Again, the model should resemble the photo. Turn the model over.

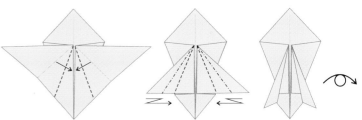

4 Check to be sure that you have the correct side of the paper by looking at the center line: it should be a valley-fold. Open up the model, then valley-fold the top corner to the center of the bottom edge of the model. Valley-fold this square corner piece way back, toward the top of the model. Notice the black dots at the end of the crease lines in the diagram. Align the end of each of the two crease lines with the folded edge of paper on their way up (dot-to-dot in the diagram). This will show you how far to fold the corner back up.

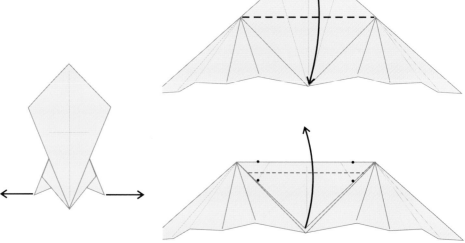

5 Create a scalloped edge along the bottom of the wings by setting in the indicated mountain- and valley-folds (optional). Mountain-fold the left and right arm-edges (see the circle diagram for detail) under and out of sight.

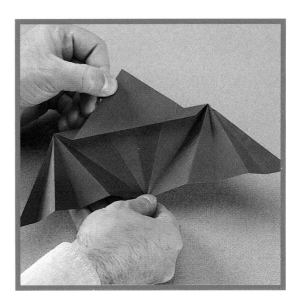

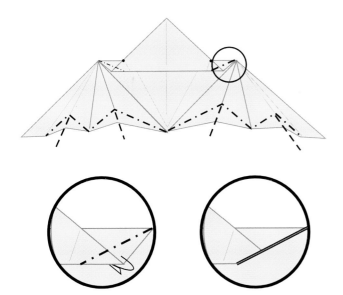

6 Mountain- and valley-fold the top corner to make the nose and head. Fold the nose first and then valley-fold the whole shape down. Fold the wings closed over the body. Use the diagram in Step 7 as a guide.

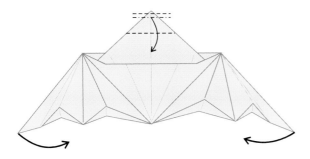

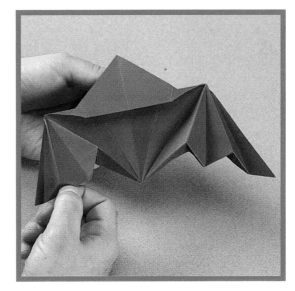

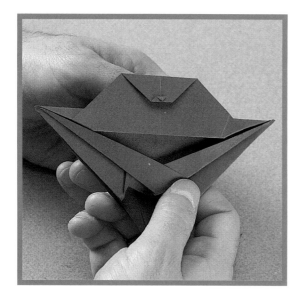

7 Mountain-fold the arms in half, lengthwise, beginning from the corner point and working inward until you hit a mountain-crease in the area of the body. Swing this mountain-crease up to touch the nearest ear corner and valley-fold the paper between them.

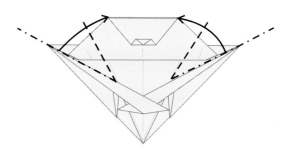

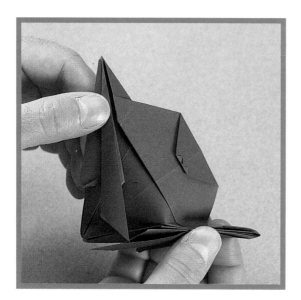

8 The folding of the previous step defines the head area and supplies material for shaping the features.

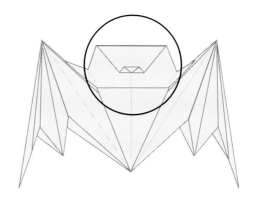

9 Mountain-fold along the paper edge that runs from ear point to ear point. Valley-fold the two ear points across the top of the head and make them stand straight up.

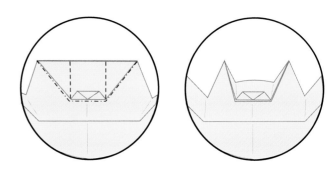

10 Twist the ear points so that the flat sides face forward (optional). Open the mouth using a toothpick or similar tool (also optional).

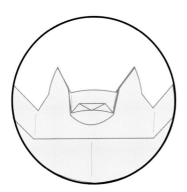

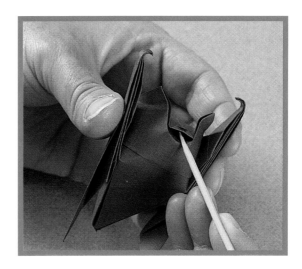

11 Open the wings out and tightly curl the end of each wing around a toothpick to shape. You may wish to make a few roosting bats by folding the wings closed.

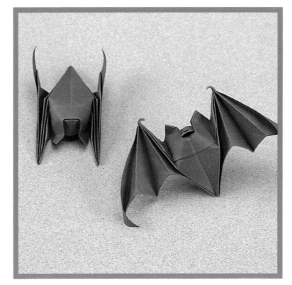

A paper frog brooch makes a simple accessory that is suitable for all ages.

Paper Animals Gallery

Colorful, tropical parrots are perfect as tree ornaments, and will brighten anybody's day.

Use the Sea Turtle Box as a party favor and a friendly surprise filled with treats.

Make an authentic bat mobile! These excellent models are cheerful and friendly, hardly the types to cause alarm.

Try using a paper frog on a lily pad as a package ornament. Adding a paper frog is a quick and easy way to make any gift more fun.

The segmented bodies of toy paper lizards wiggle when handled. They make great accent pieces for a southwestern- or tropical-theme parties, and are lots of fun at children's birthday parties, too.

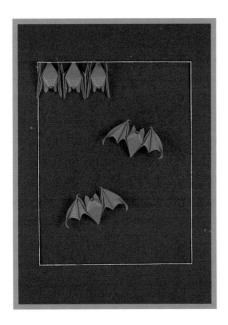

An elegant arrangement of good-luck bats in a framed wall hanging. Bats and the color red are both highly regarded by the Chinese as symbols of good luck.

Arrange fancy ornamental koi on a tabletop, or create a beautiful mobile of colorful, swimming koi. The river stones pictured are actually examples of raku, a Japanese ceramic glaze technique. Stones created by Paul Rossi, Essex, New York.

Adorn the lid of a simple jewelry box with a zebra and her colt; or substitute horses or ponies for equestrian-minded friends.

About the Author

Michael G. LaFosse, origami artist and papermaker, has been practicing the art of paper folding for more than 25 years. He teaches, designs, and works as a consultant to museums and schools. His work has been exhibited in galleries and museums throughout the United States.

LaFosse's interest in paper folding began at the age of 7. At the age of 12, he was inspired to begin creating his own original designs after seeing the extraordinary origami art of Japanese master Akira Yoshizawa. He has since had the opportunity to visit Japan and study with Yoshizawa.

Origami designs by LaFosse have been featured in books, film, computer programs, and in designer displays at Symphony Hall in Boston and at SAKS Fifth Avenue in New York. His original designs for this series blend origami, paper construction, and special folding techniques to produce elegant results. Through workshops, videos, and finding new venues for showing his work, LaFosse is bringing the ancient art of origami to a widening audience.

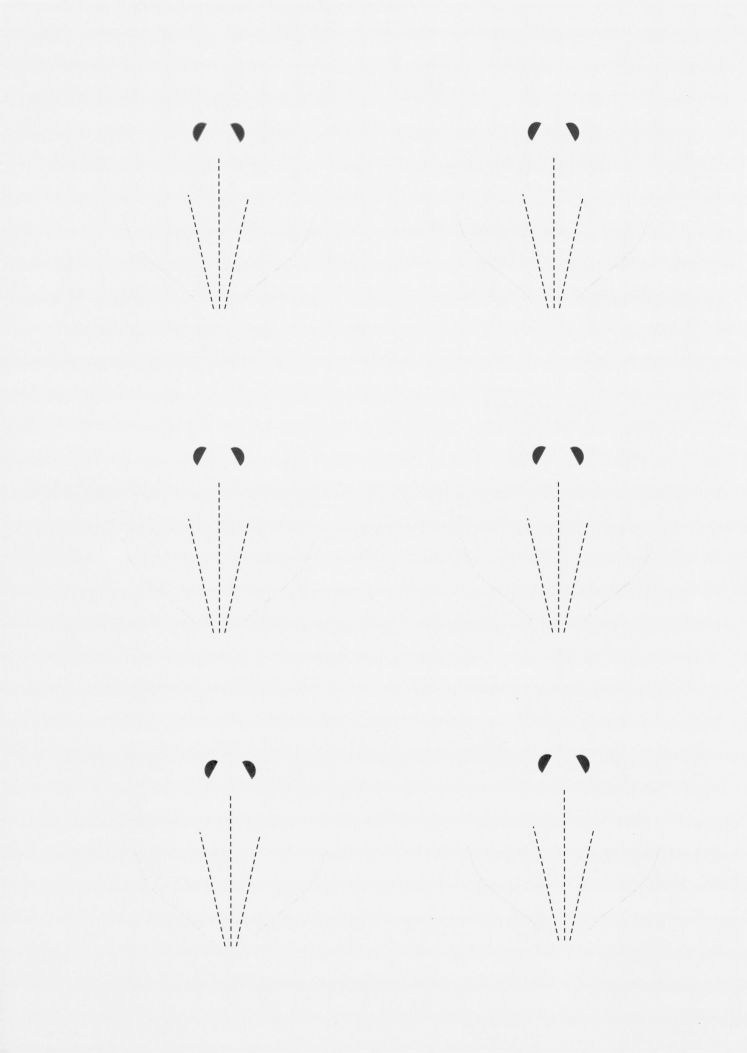

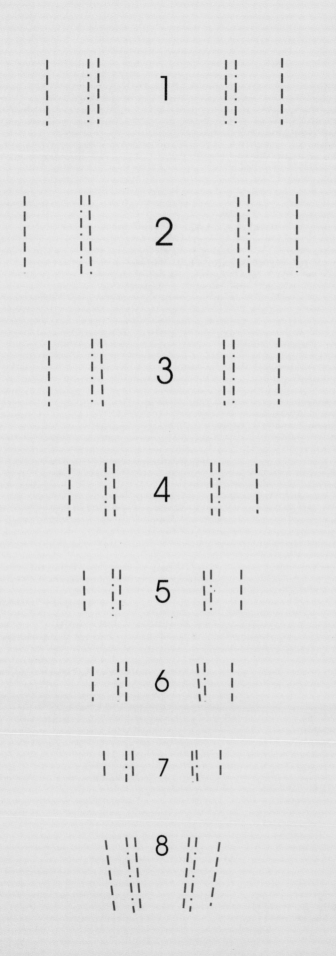

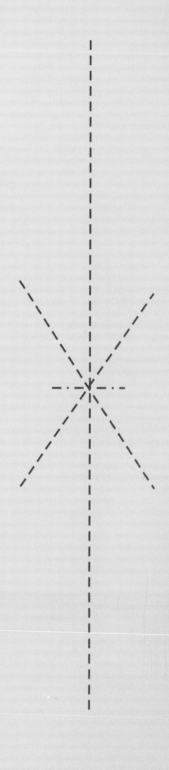

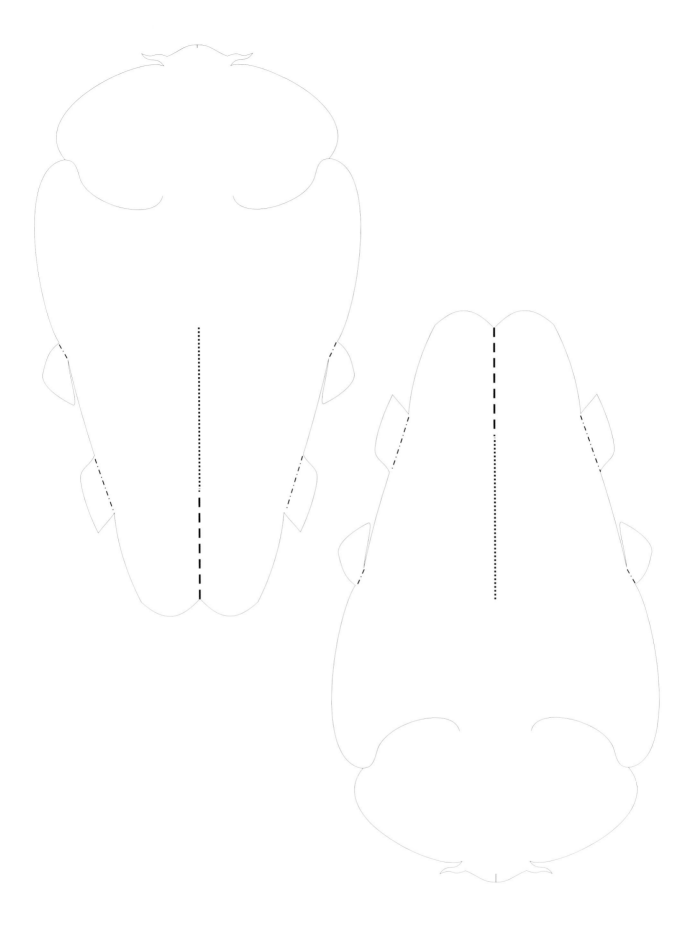

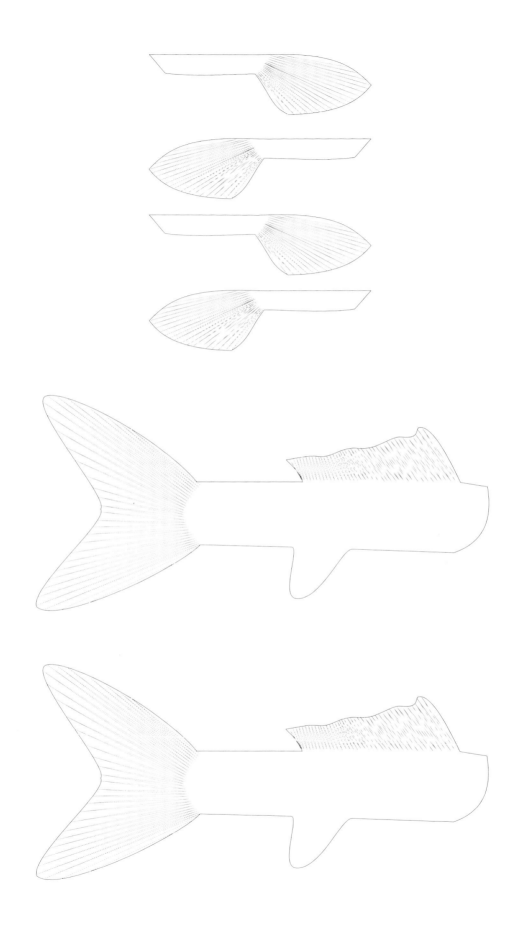

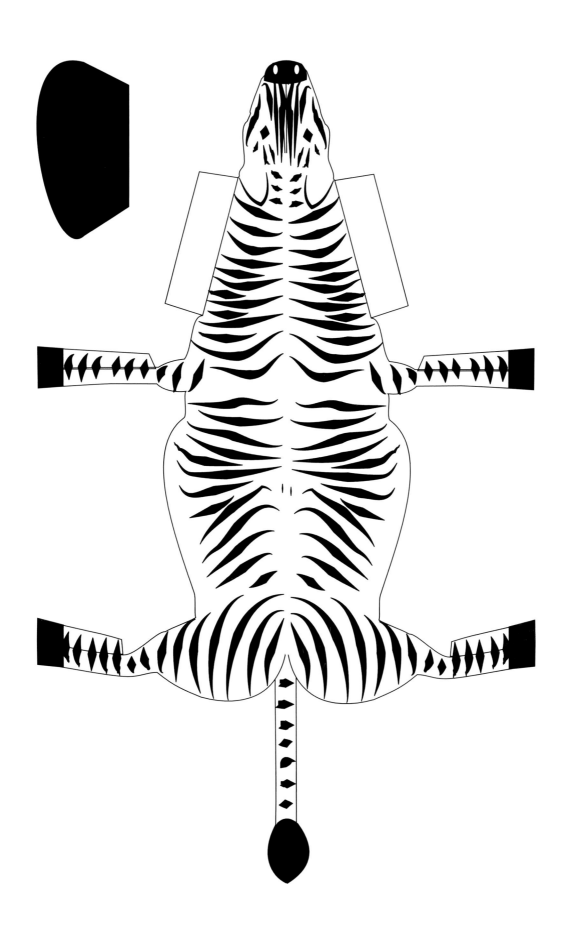

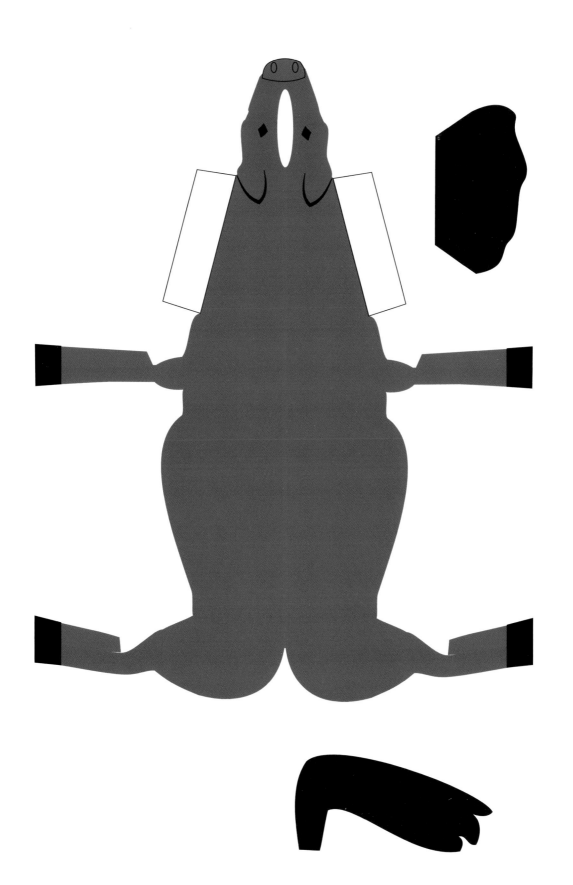

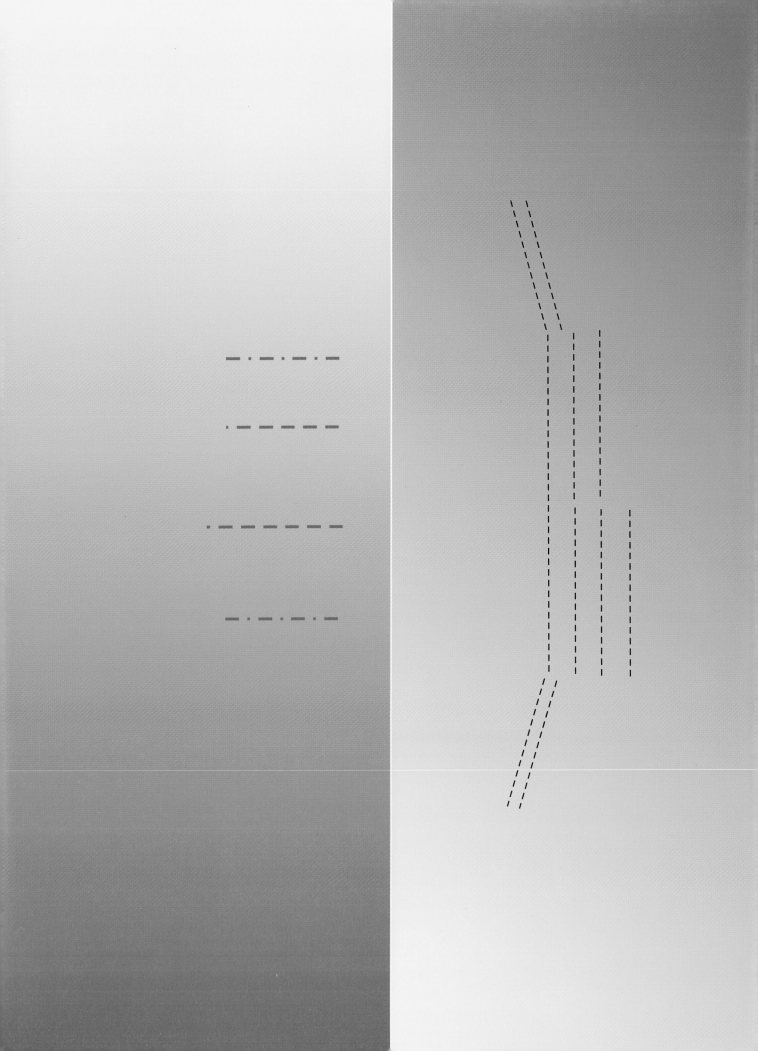

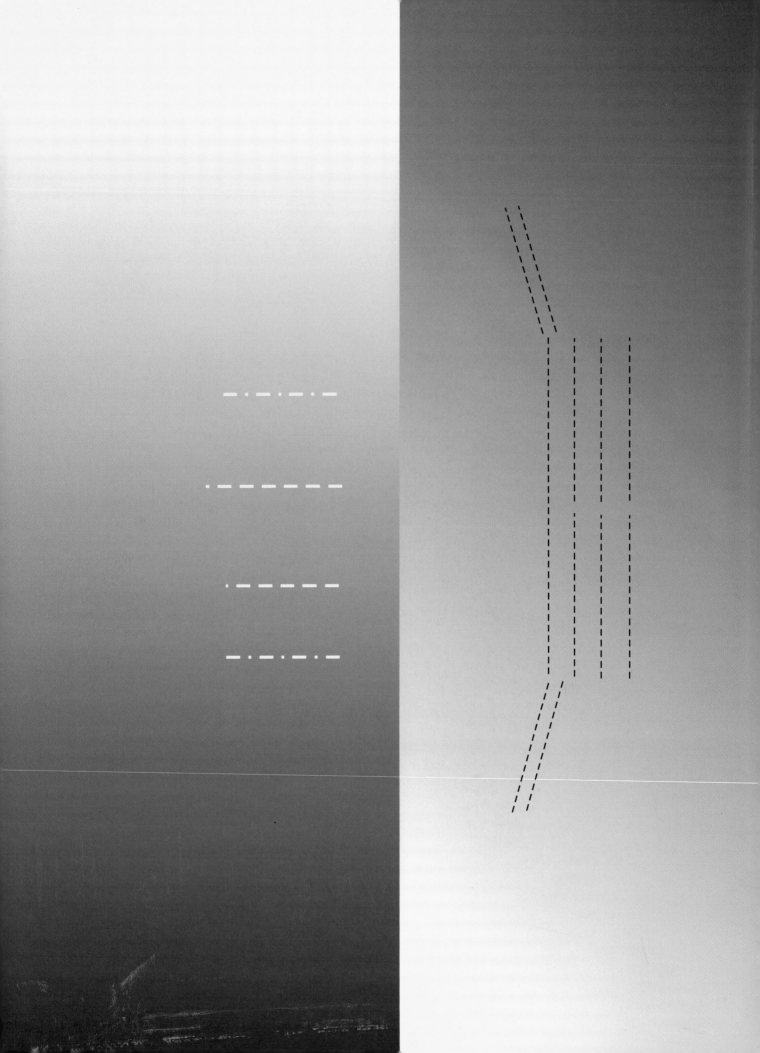

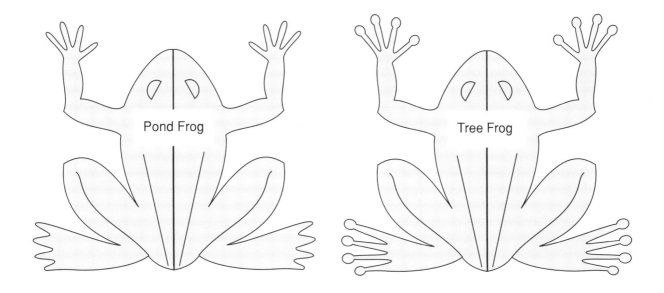

Pond Frog

Tree Frog

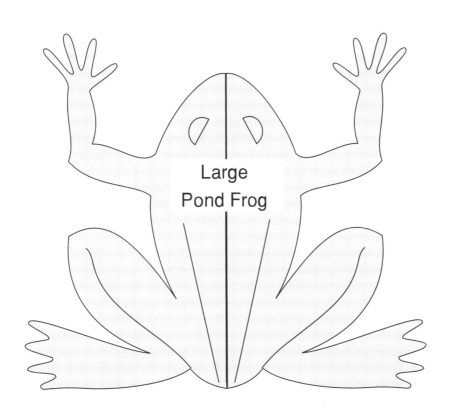

Large
Pond Frog

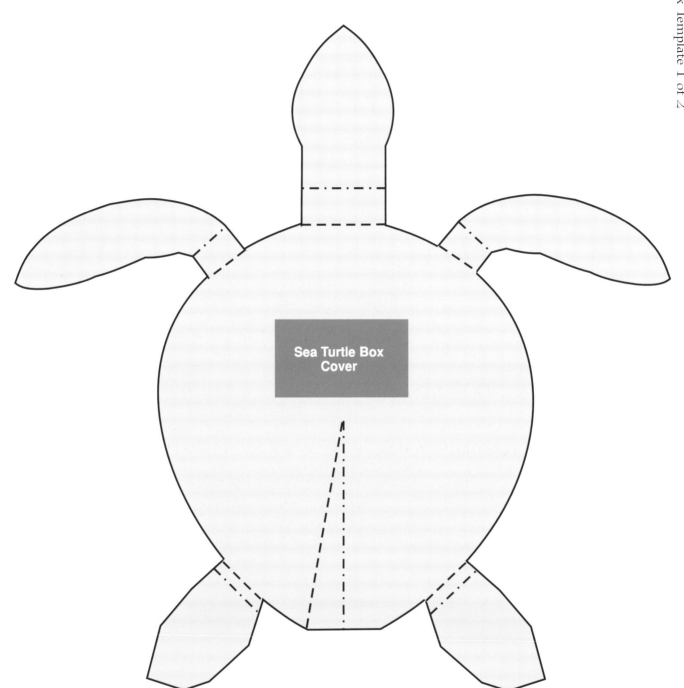

Sea Turtle Box
Cover

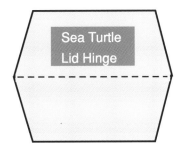

Sea Turtle
Lid Hinge

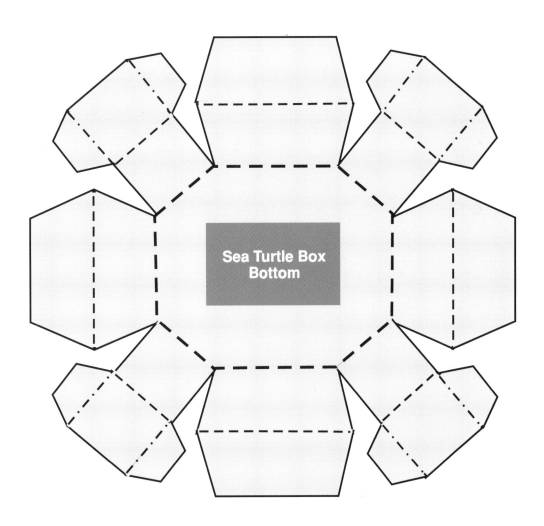

Sea Turtle Box
Bottom

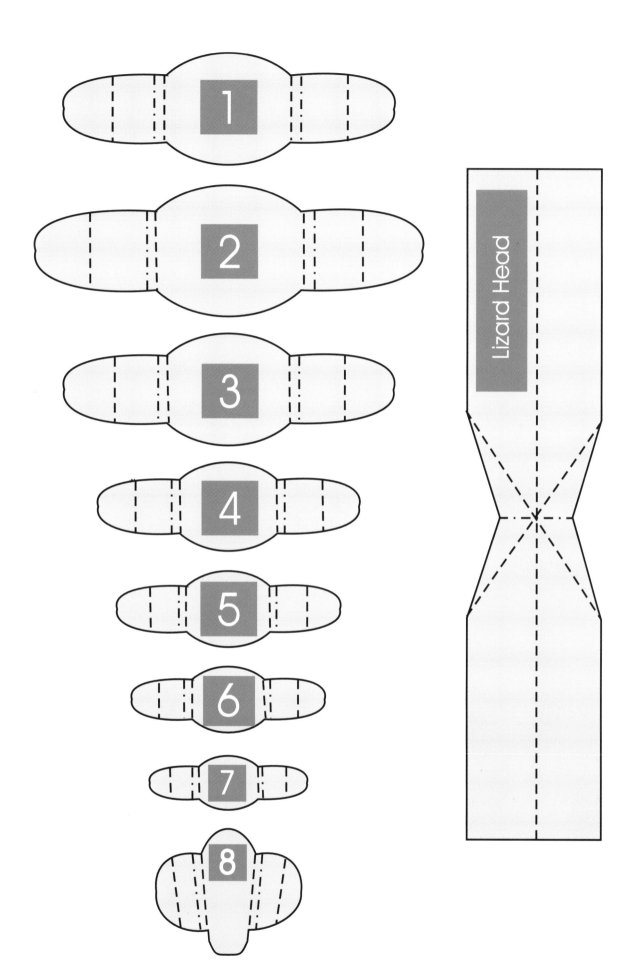

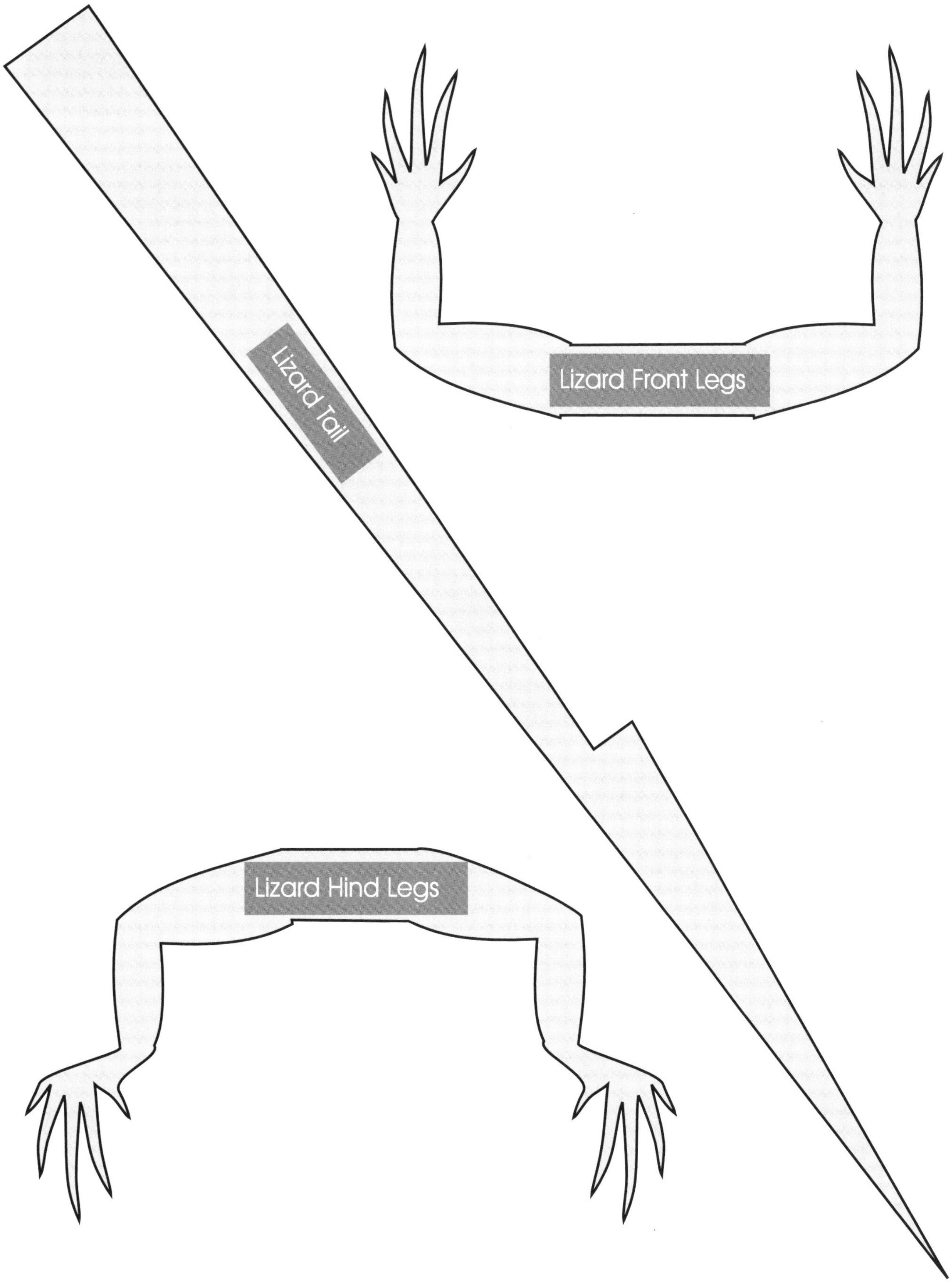

Lizard Tail

Lizard Front Legs

Lizard Hind Legs

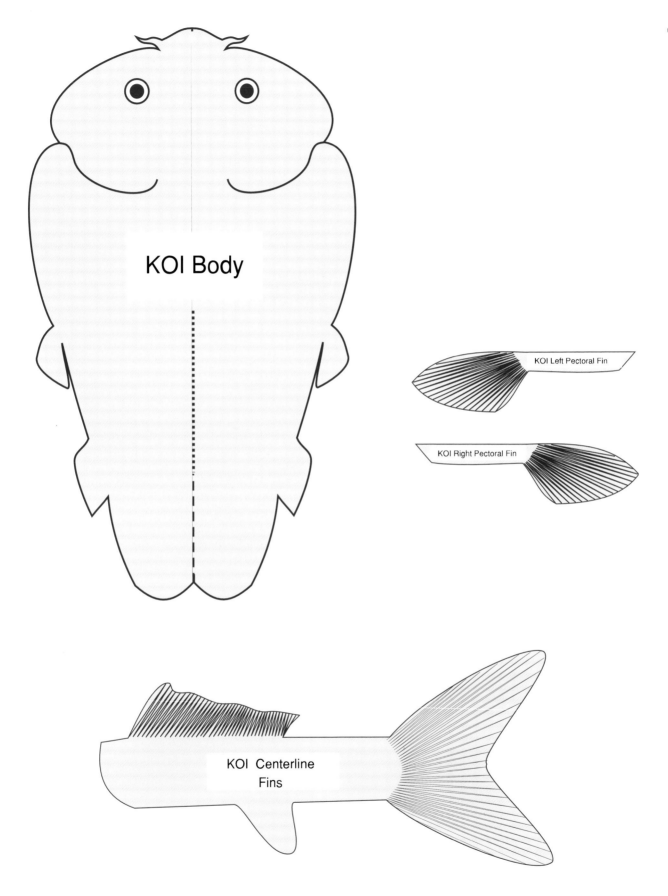

KOI Body

KOI Left Pectoral Fin

KOI Right Pectoral Fin

KOI Centerline
Fins

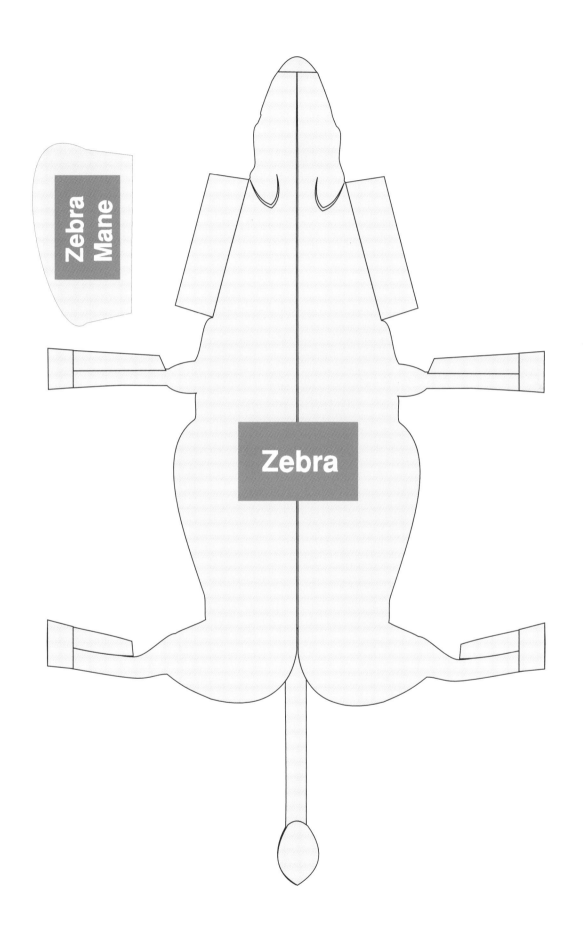

Zebra
Mane

Zebra

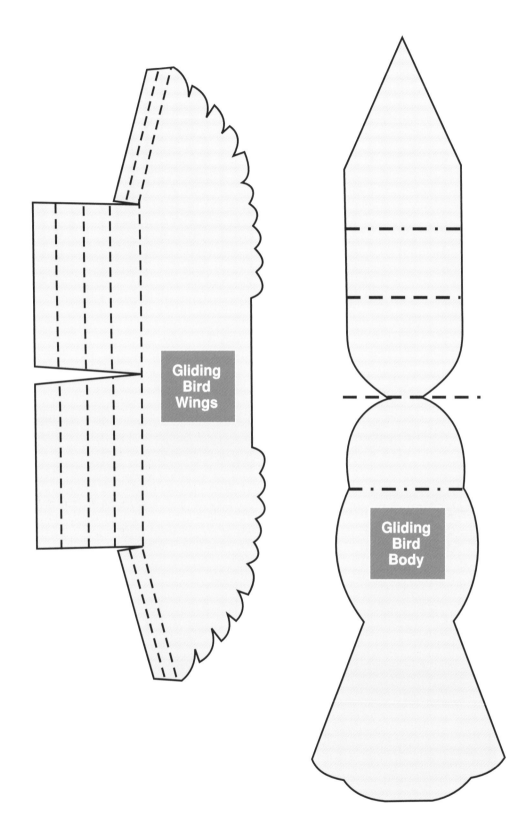

Gliding Bird Wings

Gliding Bird Body

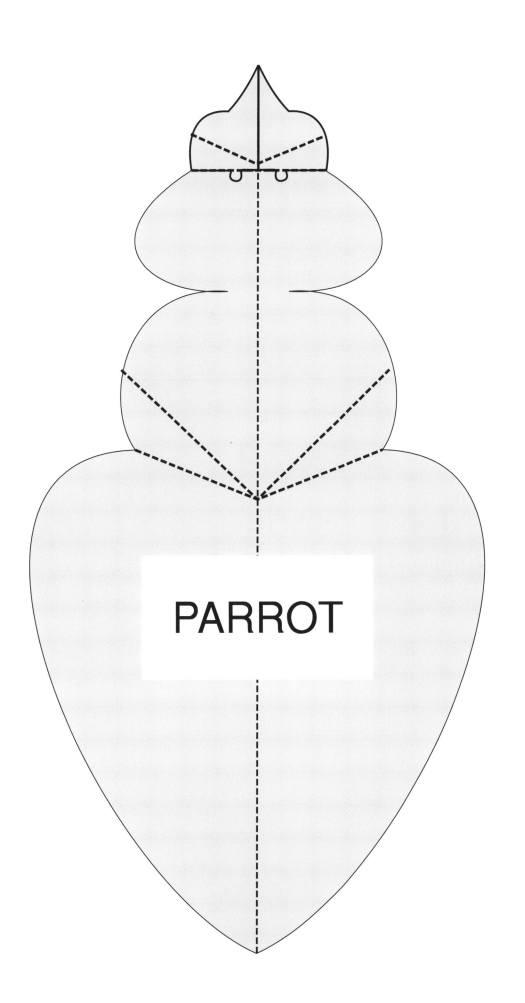

PARROT

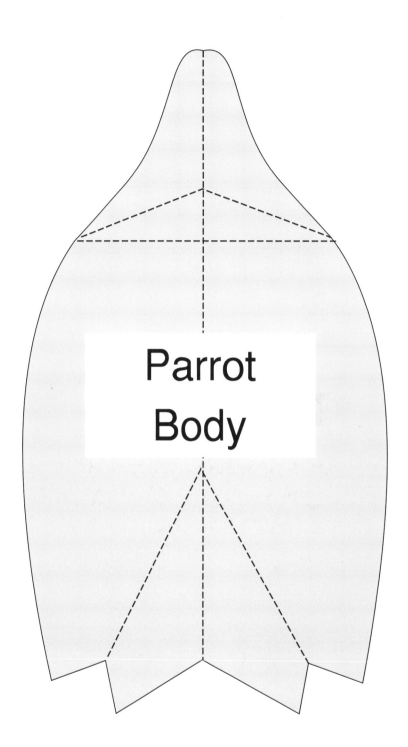

Parrot
Body

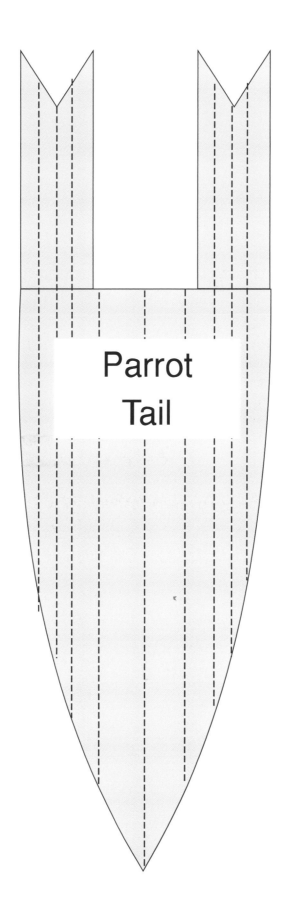

Parrot
Tail